trotman

REAL LIFE ISSUES:
PREJUDICE

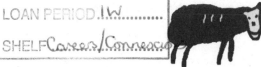

Rozina Breen

Real Life Issues: Prejudice
This first edition published in 2006 by Trotman and Company Ltd
2 The Green, Richmond, Surrey TW9 1PL

Editorial and Publishing Team
Author Rozina Breen
Editorial Mina Patria, Editorial Director; Rachel Lockhart, Commissioning Editor;
Catherine Travers, Managing Editor; Ian Turner, Editorial Assistant
Production Ken Ruskin, Head of Manufacturing and Logistics;
James Rudge, Production Artworker
Sales and Marketing Suzanne Johnson, Marketing Manager
Advertising Tom Lee, Commercial Director

Designed by XAB

British Library Cataloguing in Publication Data
A catalogue record for this book is available from the British Library

ISBN 1 84455 101 6

Typeset by Photoprint, Torquay
Printed and bound in Great Britain by Cromwell Press, Trowbridge, Wiltshire

CONTENTS:

'We all have a responsibility to question what we are taught and to challenge our own preconceptions.'

REAL LIFE ISSUES:
Prejudice

ABOUT THE AUTHOR

Rozina Breen worked as a senior producer for the BBC's Current Affairs unit in London until 2004. She worked on a variety of programmes for BBC1, BBC2, Radio 4 and also 5 Live. She studied English and Drama at University College of Wales, Aberystwyth and also obtained a Master's degree from the University of Leeds. She is currently an employment analyst, looking specifically at gender equality issues for women in science, engineering and technology. She lives in Yorkshire with her husband and three young children.

REAL LIFE ISSUES:
Prejudice

ACKNOWLEDGEMENTS

Heartfelt thanks to the following for their time, knowledge and expertise: Jared O'Mara, British Council for Disabled People; Marc Lorenzi, Leeds Racial Harassment Project; Phillip Hodson, Fellow of the British Association for Counselling and Psychotherapy; Families and Friends of Lesbians and Gays (FFLAG); Stonewall; Joint Action Against Homophobic Bullying; Andrew Edwards, BBC broadcaster and media lecturer at Trinity and All Saints College, Leeds; Muslim Council of Britain (MCB); the British Dyslexia Association; the National Autistic Society; KidsHealth and the Nemours Foundation.

For their love and support, thanks to Davey, Shay, Jakey, Laily and, as always, to Rumina.

This book is dedicated to all those who have been touched by prejudice. May your courage continue to inspire.

INTRODUCTION

Prejudice is all around us; there's no getting away from it. If we're completely honest with ourselves, we all have prejudices of one sort or another. And we are all likely to be on the receiving end of prejudice or discriminatory behaviour at some point in our lives.

Prejudice is never right. It stems from fear and simply not understanding what it's like to be that other person. It is an enormous and complicated subject. The first three chapters of this book will take you through the issues, answering questions like:

- What is the difference between prejudice and discrimination?
- Why are people prejudiced?
- Which groups are people prejudiced against?
- How do people show their prejudice?
- What does it feel like when people are prejudiced against you?

Prejudice can come from many sources – your peers, your parents, your school, public organisations and even yourself. And it can be directed at many different people. Chapters 4–8 look at some of the groups about which people most commonly form prejudiced opinions.

But, although it might seem a huge mountain to climb, prejudice can be overcome. By understanding why people discriminate, and how the situation can be managed, we hope you will begin to feel more positive and more able to deal with the situations you find yourself in.

> *'We are all likely to be on the receiving end of prejudice or discriminatory behaviour at some point in our lives.'*

Chapter 9 and the Helpful Organisations section at the end of this book offer tips and coping methods and list support groups who can help you if you feel you have nowhere else to turn. Remember that you are not alone and prejudice is something you don't have to deal with by yourself. We hope that this book will show you how to see the light at the end of the tunnel.

CHAPTER ONE

WHAT IS PREJUDICE?
What does being prejudiced mean? Who is prejudiced? And who are they prejudiced against?

Have you ever felt that someone judged you before even taking the time to get to know you? If so, then you have experienced prejudice. The word prejudice is the noun relating to the verb 'to **prejudge**', which means forming an opinion before you have all the facts.

There are lots of examples of prejudice in the world, some of which you might come across at school, at home or on the television. It's unfair – and sad – that prejudice exists so widely. This chapter will look at what prejudice actually is and show how easy it can be to make generalisations about groups of people without getting to know them.

EXAMPLES OF PREJUDICE
You may have heard others saying things like this about whole groups:

- 'All Italians are ...'
- 'Jews always ...'
- 'Girls can't ...'
- 'Gay people always ...'
- 'Old people are ...'

When people say something like this, they are dealing in **stereotypes**. A stereotype is a preconceived or oversimplified generalisation about an entire group of people without regard for their individual differences. (Stereotypes can be positive as well as negative.) They happen when someone's contact with a certain group of people has been limited, and so their opinions are built on false assumptions. For example, someone's limited knowledge of Muslims or black people may lead them to say something like:

■ 'All Muslims wear long black clothes.'
■ 'All black people can dance.'

Similarly, someone who has never visited the UK may say something like:

■ 'All English people drink tea all the time.'
■ 'All British people are white.'

WHO ARE WE PREJUDICED AGAINST?

As the examples above show, people are generally prejudiced against others who aren't the same as they are. For example, they may pick on those who aren't the same colour as them, those who have a different faith, or those who have a different sexuality. (Chapters 4–8 of this book look in more depth at some of the different groups against which people are often prejudiced.)

Difference and diversity

But if you look around you, everyone is different in one way or another. We live in a country filled with diversity and variety – millions of people with different religions, beliefs and languages. You can see that in a classroom, at the supermarket, on TV, or just walking down the street.

Think about how boring life might be if everyone in your street and neighbourhood were the same. Living in communities that include different races and cultures and people with varied abilities and behaviours can add a lot to our everyday experiences, making our lives richer and more interesting. For example, look at the way India has influenced fashion in the UK – and think about how many people from a non-Indian background love to go out for a curry or listen to bhangra music.

> 'Think about how boring life might be if everyone in your street and neighbourhood were the same.'

In order to overcome prejudice, we need to break down the stereotypical views in people's heads – and a very good way of doing this is by living in communities where you regularly meet different types of people. This is covered in more detail in Chapter 9.

The law

As the world becomes more diverse, so the law has changed to protect people against prejudice. All prejudice and discrimination goes against the first two Articles of the United Nations Declaration of Human Rights:

- **Article 1:** All human beings are born free and equal in dignity and rights. They are endowed with reason and conscience and should act towards one another in a spirit of brotherhood.
- **Article 2:** Everyone is entitled to all the rights and freedoms set forth in this Declaration, without distinction of any kind, such as race, colour, sex, language, religion, political or other opinion, national or social origin, property, birth or other status.

WE ALL HAVE PREJUDICES

There are many different reasons why people develop prejudiced opinions and, if we look deep enough, we'll find that we all have prejudices of one sort or another. It could be that we don't like people who are large, who smoke, who dye their hair or who wear certain types of clothes. Try the quiz below to investigate whether you have some stereotyped or prejudiced views.

Think about your reactions. Are they positive or negative? Where do your ideas and opinions come from? Think about how easy it is to create an instant picture of someone simply from a label.

QUIZ

Write down the first thing you think of when you hear the following:

1. 'Old age pensioner'
2. 'Disabled teenager'
3. 'Muslim girl'
4. 'Autistic boy'.

Now read the points below:

1. Do you see the old age pensioner as infirm and housebound? Or do you imagine someone who is still very youthful and travelling the world?
2. Do you picture the disabled person in a wheelchair or as someone who can't speak up for themselves? Or do you imagine a popular classmate who DJs at night?
3. What about the Muslim girl – is she wearing a hijab (a headscarf) or a burka (a garment covering her face and perhaps

---

also her whole body) and speaking a different language? Or has she changed into her casual clothes, wearing jeans and a t-shirt, having a laugh with her friends, some of whom are white, some black and some Asian? Did you know that a Muslim's choice of dress is largely cultural and there are many variations?

4 And what about the autistic boy – is he doing something on his own in the corner of the classroom? Or is he telling you something interesting?

It's worth thinking about your own prejudices and trying to steer clear of those images that instantly come into your head. Make sure you take the time to learn about a person for who they really are, rather than what they may seem to represent. You can find out more about how to avoid being prejudiced in Chapter 9.

Are we a prejudiced nation?

Research about prejudice in the UK has shown where our prejudices lie, revealing which groups are most discriminated against and what influences people to be prejudiced. The charity Stonewall has carried out a project called Citizenship 21. Using research from MORI, it reported that almost two out of three adults named at least one minority group towards whom they felt less positive – that's a massive **25 million adults across England who admit they are prejudiced towards a certain group of people**.

People were asked which groups they felt less positive about:

- 35% said travellers and Gypsies
- 34% said refugees and asylum seekers
- 18% said people from a different ethnic group
- 17% said gay or lesbian people.

They were also asked which groups of people they felt were most likely to experience discrimination in society.

- 50% said asylum seekers
- 49% said people from ethnic minorities
- 38% said travellers and Gypsies
- 37% said gay or lesbian people
- 24% said physically disabled people
- 19% said people with learning disabilities.

Forty-three per cent said they knew personally someone who was prejudiced against people from a different ethnic group to their own; 35% knew someone who was prejudiced against gay and lesbian people.

Prejudice is a pattern of thinking, so people who are prejudiced against one group of people are often prejudiced against many others too. This is known as 'joined-up' prejudice.

FACT BOX

People who are prejudiced against an ethnic group are twice as likely to be prejudiced against gay and lesbian people, and people who discriminate on the basis of race are four times as likely to be prejudiced against disabled people.

Source: Stonewall

CONCLUSION

Prejudice is a mindset based on generalisations and stereotypes – and it is surprising how easy it is to become prejudiced. However, prejudice is only a thought or a feeling in someone's head. When someone allows their prejudice to influence the way they behave, they move from prejudice to discrimination. The next chapter will look at the different ways people discriminate against those they are prejudiced against, and it will also look at some of the reasons why this happens.

HOW AND WHY DO PEOPLE DISCRIMINATE?

What types of behaviour are associated with prejudice? Where do we get our prejudiced opinions from?

WHAT IS DISCRIMINATION?

People sometimes say that **discrimination = prejudice + power**. Discrimination happens when people act on their prejudices; when they 'show' their prejudice by allowing a prejudiced thought pattern or opinion to influence their behaviour.

HOW DO PEOPLE DISCRIMINATE?

As you will see later in this chapter, there are so many different reasons for people's prejudices that they can show their discrimination in many different ways. The book *Understanding Prejudice* outlines some common types of discriminatory behaviour:

- **Aggressive** – often carried out by racists and backed with threats of violence, usually against asylum-seekers, travellers and Gypsies
- **Banal** – unintentional bigotry by people ignorant of political correctness, for example calling gay people 'queer', which passes unnoticed
- **Benevolent** – this is typified by pitying comments, often by do-gooders, for example towards disabled people, which are intended positively but which label them as vulnerable or helpless
- **Cathartic** – used by people to justify their bigoted views, such as a customer who makes a racist comment because he thinks an Asian shopkeeper has slighted him
- **Unintentional** – unwitting ignorance that shows a lack of understanding of diversity and rights. Used, for example, by people who think gays are 'nice' but who may look down on them or fail to take their relationships seriously.

(Source: *Understanding Prejudice* by Professor Gill Valentine, Sheffield University and Ian McDonald, Brighton University)

Discrimination can be obvious (for example someone might shout nasty things or physically attack you) – but it can also be less obvious (for example you could be stared at or simply ignored). If you are being subjected to discrimination then it is quite likely that you will experience both the more and the less obvious types of discriminatory behaviour, in the form of bullying and exclusion.

Bullying

Bullying is a common form of behaviour associated with prejudice. Examples of bullying behaviour are:

- Being called names
- Being teased or made fun of in front of other people
- Being talked to in a patronising manner

■ Having rumours spread about you
■ Being hit or kicked
■ Having your belongings stolen.

It can take over your life and make you not want to go to school. It can affect your confidence and self-esteem, and it can make you feel frightened and unhappy about many things in your life.

CASE STUDY

Shamila, 15, called Childline in tears saying that she dreaded going to school. She told her counsellor how she used to be outgoing but she 'didn't like talking much now'. For the past month Shamila had been bullied by a gang of girls in her class because, she said, 'I'm the only Asian girl in my school'. Shamila explained that she couldn't talk to her parents about how she was feeling because her mum and dad were not getting on very well and she didn't want to add to their worries.

It is important to remember that bullying is never right – and, as Shamila's case shows, even if you do not feel you can talk to your family, there are other people out there who can help and support you. You do not have to deal with bullies on your own – Chapter 9 and the Helpful Organisations section at the end of this book will give you some tips on coping and some ideas on who to turn to.

> **For a closer look at bullying,**
> **see *Real Life Issues: Bullying.***

Exclusion

If you are stared at, ignored or made to feel that you can't join in then you are being excluded. This kind of discriminatory behaviour can be quite subtle and nothing specific may ever be said out loud: everything may be expressed through body language alone (especially through eye contact).

As well as making you feel socially isolated, exclusion also has other implications, because it is not just your peers at school who can exclude you. You might feel there are low expectations from your family, teachers or other people around you – often because they have already made up their minds about what you want to do, what you can do and what you can't do – all based on a stereotype.

> *'Exclusion to me simply means that many people have little chance of fulfilling their potential because of prejudicial barriers.'*
>
> **Phillip Hodson, Counsellor**

WHY DO PEOPLE DISCRIMINATE?

People discriminate because they are prejudiced. And prejudice is born from:

- Jealousy
- Fear and insecurity
- Ignorance
- Desire for power
- A strong belief that we should all be the same.

This is partly down to an ancient tribal instinct: on some level we are programmed to prefer 'our own kind' – people we can understand and identify with. But it is also about fear – whether fear of losing privileges, power, jobs, money, social identity or control.

Beneath all of this lies a psychological insecurity – no one would wish to belittle someone else if they felt really strong inside themselves. Some people who feel unimportant or bad about themselves think they will feel better if they pick on or bully others. Sometimes, people who say these things are angry or upset, and they want to lash out. But if you are being discriminated against, always remember: **there is no excuse for prejudice. It's not your fault**.

'No one would wish to belittle someone else if they felt really strong inside themselves.'

WHERE DO THESE ATTITUDES COME FROM?

We have seen that prejudice is born from jealousy, fear and the belief that we should all be the same – but what makes some people think this way? There are many factors influencing our opinions – and two of the strongest are our upbringing and the media.

Inherited attitudes

The home environment is the greatest influence for our own beliefs and attitudes. It's not surprising that we take as gospel the things our parents tell us – they helped us learn to eat, walk, read and write, so why should we question the things they tell us about people around us? If we hear prejudiced comments while growing up – either from family or from friends – it may seem hard not to copy them.

The media

Although family influences are the main reason for our beliefs and attitudes, the media also has a part to play in shaping the way we

FACT BOX

One in three people say their prejudiced views are learned from their parents; one in four say they are learned from TV and newspapers.

Source: Stonewall

think. What we read about in magazines and see on TV can reinforce certain stereotypes.

Look at the images on your TV screen, on posters around you and in newspapers and magazines. How do they reflect your experiences? Are there enough black and Asian people in the soaps? Do the magazines you read ever talk about learning disabilities?

Gary Younge, a writer for the *Guardian* newspaper, has said that the media still has a long way to go in reflecting the ethnic make-up of Britain. He observed that even in the late 1990s, 'most of the black people you see in the newspaper cafeterias are serving the food'.

Interview with Andrew Edwards

Andrew Edwards presents an all-speech, weekday breakfast show on BBC Radio Leeds. He also teaches radio at Trinity and All Saints College in Leeds.

Did the media rely on stereotypes in the past?
'We used to rely too much on lazy stereotypes. White, middle-class, middle-aged men in suits often seemed to be the easiest to track down as interviewees or guests for programmes. We tended to stick with the regular names in our contact books

rather than looking for people we hadn't spoken to before. It wasn't so much a case of active discrimination, more that we didn't think enough of wider issues. Who are we broadcasting to? Does what we're talking about interest our listeners? Do the voices we hear on air reflect the wider population?'

Has the media been forced to change?
'I think society in general is growing up. Many of us live in multi-cultural communities. The sort of casual racist language or abuse of people with learning disabilities – once common – is simply no longer acceptable.'

Does the media still use stereotypes?
'Of course there are still stereotypes. Tabloid newspapers are full of them – the high-flying businesswoman who tries to have it all by having a family or the "plucky have-a-go hero" who takes on a street criminal. Think how often we see the Asian family running a corner shop on a television news bulletin. Do we, as often, see the Asian family as successful entrepreneurs or teachers in an inner-city school?'

Why is the media so powerful in shaping the way we think?
'[It is] powerful because so much of our view of the world comes through the filter of the media: the attitudes expressed, the people we see, the subjects discussed, the clothes worn, the sports covered. Think of the magazines you read – how much do they shape what you think, buy and wear? The answer – whether it's an MTV show, a tabloid showbiz column or a Radio 1 DJ – is, in the widest sense, the media. That's why the range of people we talk to, see and interview and the spread of views represented are so important.'

'We all have a responsibility to question what we are taught and to challenge our own preconceptions in order to make sure that we never contribute to the problem.'

CONCLUSION

For some people, prejudice may be the result of the influences they have been subjected to in the home or in the media – you could say that they are prejudiced simply because they don't know any better. However, this is not really an excuse: as you will see in the next chapter, the effects of the discriminatory behaviour outlined above can be extremely upsetting and therefore we all have a responsibility to question what we are taught and to challenge our own preconceptions in order to make sure that we never contribute to the problem. Chapter 9 explores some ways of doing this.

CHAPTER THREE

HOW DOES DISCRIMINATION MAKE US FEEL?
What emotions might you experience? Could there be other knock-on effects?

THE INITIAL EFFECTS

If you are being subjected to discrimination, you might feel:

- Hurt
- Angry
- Embarrassed
- Confused
- Frustrated
- Alone
- Threatened
- Excluded
- Exposed
- Scared
- Worried.

THE KNOCK-ON EFFECTS

Experiencing all these emotions is upsetting and stressful – and it may also mean that you begin to respond to situations differently, although you may not even realise that this is happening.

For example, if some of your classmates are bullying you because of your disability, you may find that, when you meet new people (who have not ever bullied you), you are no longer able to **trust** them.

You may find yourself on the **defensive** all the time, always thinking 'What do you want?' or 'What's your evil game?'. You may feel that you always have to justify your actions and find yourself constantly waiting for people to criticise you – even if they don't.

This can make you overly **critical of yourself** – because after a while, even someone with the most robust personality will start to wonder whether there might be some justification for the way people are treating them (even though they know, at least in theory, that there never is). This can lead to **low self-esteem** – which means that you no longer value yourself or appreciate your own worth and importance. (Someone with healthy self-esteem is able to feel good about themselves and take pride in their abilities, skills and accomplishments.)

> **For a closer look at self-esteem,**
> see *Real Life Issues: Confidence and Self-Esteem.*

It may also lead you to ask yourself 'How can I change?' – because it seems as though the only way to overcome the problem is to fit in and 'be normal'. This can cause feelings of **guilt**, because you know that the things you want to change are actually a very important part of who you are – and no one should have the right to make you feel that you have to change them.

Coping with all these emotions and doubts can be extremely draining. Counsellor Phillip Hodgson explains that young people may think 'This is unfair, no action of mine merits the offence and I can't win.' It may feel like you are running a marathon just to stay in the same place, while others around you cruise past because they are not having to deal with the same issues as you. It can also lead to other mental health problems such as panic attacks, eating disorders, depression and even suicide attempts.

'It may feel like you are running a marathon just to stay in the same place.'

CONCLUSION

Experiencing discrimination is painful and unfair – and it is not an easy aspect of our lives to face. But remember that you don't have to deal with it alone: talking to support groups, friends, teachers and others who have experienced it is a good way of helping you get on top of the situation. And there are lots of coping mechanisms to help you through the most difficult periods and show you there is a way forward – these are explained in Chapter 9.

The following chapters outline in more detail the particular issues surrounding race, religion, sexuality, disability and learning differences – and look at why these are particularly rich areas for those with prejudices to feed off.

CHAPTER FOUR:

RACISM
*What is racism
and how can
you cope with it?*

WHAT IS RACISM?

A racist is someone who picks on someone else, treats them
differently or considers them inferior because of their colour, ethnic
background, culture, country of origin, religion or language.

Some different types of racism are:

- Anti-Semitism (prejudice against someone because they are Jewish)
- Islamophobia (prejudice against someone because they are Muslim
  – see page 26 for more information)
- Sectarianism (strong devotion to a particular form of religion, often
  leading to prejudice against other beliefs).

Refugees, asylum seekers, Irish travellers and Gypsies also all
experience discrimination and racism.

Being judged by someone's misguided or stereotypical opinions about
your race, religion and culture can be very difficult to deal with. This
chapter examines some of the reasons for this type of discrimination

FACT BOX

For every person of non-white ethnic origin in England (3.5 million people) there are at least two who feel less positive towards them.

Source: Stonewall's Citizenship 21 Project

and looks in detail at two of the groups which suffer particularly from discrimination in this country – Muslims and refugees.

BACKGROUND

An age-old problem

Racism has existed across the world for hundreds of years (perhaps more).

At the end of the fourteenth century Europeans started to take people from Africa against their will, using them as servants or slaves for the rich and as free labour to work the sugar plantations. Slavery in America only ended in 1865 – and even then, some states had their own laws that made sure black people did not mix with white people. In most of the Southern states, marriage between black and white people was illegal and residential towns were strictly segregated into black and white areas.

Another more recent example of large-scale racism is the apartheid era in South Africa, which began in 1910. The word 'apartheid' means segregation and separation – and in South Africa, this meant that white people passed laws that allowed them to separate out, exploit and terrorise black people. In white-ruled South Africa, black people were denied basic human and political rights. In 1989 the last president of the old South African government, F W de Klerk, openly admitted the failure of apartheid policies.

Racism in the UK

In the 1950s and 1960s, when immigrants were encouraged to come to the United Kingdom to help fill jobs, life was tough. Some people had never seen non-white faces before or heard different accents from their own. As well as being suspicious of black and Asian people, they were also fearful of Irish immigrants. Trying to find a place to live, learning a new language, fitting into a new and different culture and making friends could be difficult for immigrants coming to this country.

FACT BOX

Did you know that 7.5% of the UK's population was born abroad? And, in 2001, around 4.6 million people in the United Kingdom were from non-white backgrounds.

These days the UK is a diverse, multicultural society. There are laws protecting different racial groups, and many employers are tackling the under-representation of ethnic groups in their organisations through affirmative action programmes. Nevertheless, racism is still going strong – many young people from minority ethnic or religious groups find that they are being treated differently from their friends and peers. Marc Lorenzi from the Leeds Racial Harassment Project says that 'At the ages of 12 to 15, [young people] understand why they are being treated

FACT BOX

In 2004–2005 Childline received 453 calls and letters from children about racist bullying.

differently and are becoming even more aware of the media and other institutions.'

STEPHEN LAWRENCE'S LEGACY

Stephen Lawrence was studying for his A levels when he was fatally stabbed at a bus stop near his home in Eltham, south-east London, in April 1993. A 1997 inquest ruled that he had been 'unlawfully killed in a completely unprovoked racist attack by five white youths'.

Nobody has ever been jailed for the murder and an inquiry into the failure of the first police investigation to find and convict Stephen's killers became one of the most significant events in the history of criminal justice in Britain. Sir William MacPherson, who led the inquiry, famously concluded that the police force was 'institutionally racist'. His report, published in 1999, made 70 recommendations and had an enormous impact on race relations. It led to a major change in the law, which today compels public authorities to tackle racism in a more robust manner than before.

'Stephen Lawrence's legacy is a powerful one: racism is being taken seriously and programmes put in place in an attempt to wipe it out.'

Presenting the report to Parliament, the then home secretary, Jack Straw, said, 'The Macpherson report challenges us all, not just the police service.' He expressed the determination 'to tackle discrimination wherever it is found' and emphasised that the report 'places a responsibility on each of us. We must make racial equality a reality.' The prime minister also declared his commitment to 'drive home a programme for change'.

Police forces across the country are changing, for example by recruiting officers from diverse ethnic backgrounds. Since then, other institutions have come under the spotlight for racist behaviour, including the NHS, the media and the world of football. Stephen Lawrence's legacy is a powerful one: racism is being taken seriously and programmes put in place in an attempt to wipe it out.

Balancing act

If you are lucky enough not to be suffering from the effects of prejudiced or discriminatory behaviour, it can still feel like you are walking a tight-rope, constantly struggling to balance the desire to hold on to your traditional culture and the desire to fit into mainstream society.

CASE STUDY

Ali and his family had just moved to England from Pakistan. Ali missed his friends and school back home, but he was curious about all the new things he would see and learn – and the new friends he would make. He wondered, though, whether the traditional knit skullcap that he (like many Muslims) wore would set him apart from his new classmates.

For Ali, his new life was full of change. He managed to make new friends despite being different from them. He made an effort to fit in and talked about why in some ways he was different from his classmates. He found that once he told them why he wore a skullcap, it stopped mattering. Of course, Ali and his schoolmates also had a lot in common, like football and cricket.

ISLAMOPHOBIA

There are times when one culture, race or religion will be picked out for discrimination because of current events. Recently, Muslims have been in the spotlight, particularly following the September 11 attacks in New York and the London bombings in July 2005. Some people feel suspicious of Muslims as a result of those events and – perhaps because they don't know very much about those who practise Islam – rely on negative stereotypes and myths. Prejudging Muslims in this way is known as Islamophobia. This section will look at how and why these recent events have shaped people's attitudes.

11 September

On 11 September 2001 a series of devastating attacks were launched on America. Islamic Al-Qaeda terrorists took control of four planes and crashed them into the Twin Towers of the World Trade Center in New York, the Pentagon (US military headquarters) in Washington DC and a rural area 80 miles from Pittsburgh. The attacks left almost 3000 people dead.

FACT BOX

Eight out of ten British Muslims have reported being victims of Islamophobia since 11 September.

**Islam in Britain –
Open Society Institute, 2004**

In 2005, the Commission on British Muslims and Islamophobia reported that life for the 1.6 million Muslims living in Britain has become much more difficult since the 11 September attacks in New York.

7 July

On 7 July 2005, four young British Muslim men were responsible for attacks on central London in which 52 people were killed and 700 injured. The men set off three bombs on underground trains just outside Liverpool Street and Edgware Road stations, and on another travelling between King's Cross and Russell Square. The final explosion was on a double-decker bus in Tavistock Square, not far from King's Cross.

FACT BOX

There were 269 religious hate crimes in the three weeks after 7 July 2005, compared with 40 in the same period of 2004.

Religious hate crimes, mostly against Muslims, have risen six-fold in London since the bombings, according to research by the Metropolitan Police. The Independent Race and Refugees Network lists dozens of reported cases of racist attacks following the London bombings. Most of the hate crimes consisted of verbal abuse and minor assaults, but damage to mosques and property also occurred, police said, leaving Muslims feeling uncertain and worried.

According to the Federation of Student Islamic Societies (FOSIS), before the 7 July attacks in London only 5% of those Muslim students questioned said they felt uncomfortable being Muslim in Britain. After the attacks, that figure rose to 31%.

What are the knock-on effects?

People have begun to react towards Muslims with prejudice and suspicion, which in turn makes Muslims feel isolated and marginalised. The perceived unfairness of police stop-and-searches and highly publicised anti-terrorist arrests has also led to a rise in dissatisfaction with the criminal justice system. In 2005, FOSIS stated that 'The gap between the number of stop-and-searches and that of actual arrests, charges and convictions is leading to a perception among British Muslims of being unfairly policed, and is fuelling a strong disaffection and a sense of being under siege.'

FACT BOX

Between 2001 and 2003 the number of Asians stopped and searched under the Terrorism Act 2000 increased by 302% compared with an increase of 118% for white people and 230% for black people.

Source: FOSIS 2005

Metropolitan Police Assistant Commissioner Tarique Ghaffur told the BBC that he had never seen so much anger among young Muslims. Muslim communities were particularly anxious about the increased use of stop-and-search and the new 'shoot-to-kill to protect' policy of dealing with suicide bombers, he said. 'There is no doubt that incidents affecting the Muslim community have increased.'

Muslim teenagers face a difficult time in Britain and sometimes you might feel that those around you don't really understand anything about your religion or your background.

CASE STUDY

Leyla is a Muslim teenager who lives in Gloucestershire. This is what she wrote in her article for the BBC's Where I Live website.

'Being Muslim is the most important thing in my life, because it gives me a sense of identity, it forms a framework for my life, so I know what's going to happen after I die. It also gives me a true sense of purpose for my existence on this planet.

'… I'm in my early [twenties] and I'm currently a student. My life in Gloucestershire has been great, I love the scenic surroundings and I love the fact that there aren't many Muslims here, so people are very interested in us and how we live.

'Islamophobia means, to me, the misunderstanding of Islam. I wouldn't say people are scared of Islam, but I'd say they don't understand it at all. The general public doesn't really have an outlet … where they can get information about Islam. So they read and listen to the tabloids, radio, newspapers, TV and the news programmes and assume all the information is correct.

'Islamophobia has affected me in the sense that people look at me, and the way that I'm dressed, and begin to make judgements about me. In my experience, they have [s]crewed up their faces at me and they have shouted out horrible racist things.

'Just because of what I'm wearing [it] does not class me as a terrorist, [and it] doesn't put me under any banner, whatsoever.'

What can be done?

Faith hate crimes are currently prosecuted under anti-racism legislation, but a bill to create a new offence of incitement to religious hatred is currently under discussion by the Government – there is much debate amongst all parts of the community about whether or not this is the best way to tackle the problem.

Since 11 September 2001, there has been a rise in the number of negative images of Muslims in the media, with labels such as 'fundamentalists', 'terrorists' and 'suicide bombers' being used more and more. The survey of 400 Muslim students in Britain by FOSIS also concluded that 90% feel that the way Muslims are presented in the media needs to be changed. One student commented, 'my local paper recently had a picture of Muslims praying on the front page, with the headline "Extremism hits our Town".'

'To overcome Islamophobia, people need to learn to see past the extreme stereotypes which have developed in recent years.'

If you think about it, how do your friends know what it's like to be a Muslim? Look at the media around you, at posters, magazines, newspapers and on the TV. How many positive role models are there compared to the negative images and words that surround you?

There is some work being carried out to tackle prejudice against Muslims. The government has set up a special task force to look at all the issues. To overcome Islamophobia, people need to learn to see past the extreme stereotypes which have developed in recent years, and to understand that the vast majority of Muslims are normal people with normal families and normal day-to-day problems.

But it can sometimes be hard for others to understand the culture and practices of Muslims. As they try to get to know you, you might find yourself often having to answer questions like:

- Why do you wear a skullcap?
- Why do you pray five times a day?
- What's wrong with eating pork?
- Why do you have to have an arranged marriage?
- Why do you wear a hijab?

This can seem frustrating – but it is part of the process of learning about one another.

REFUGEES AND ASYLUM SEEKERS

Refugees and asylum seekers are another group who attract a high level of prejudice and discrimination. In fact around one in three people in the UK (34% or 13.6 million adults) admits to feeling less positive towards refugees/asylum seekers. This is partly because, according to opinion polls, asylum is the third most important issue for the British public (MORI 2003) – it is rarely out of the newspapers and is the subject of often heated political and public debate. It is also because there is a huge amount of misinformation and confusion about the issues surrounding asylum. According to the Refugee Council of Great Britain, reporting and commentary about asylum seekers and refugees is often hostile, unbalanced and factually incorrect.

Setting the record straight

A **refugee** is someone who:

- Has a well-founded fear of persecution for reasons of race, religion, nationality, membership of a particular social group, or political opinion
- Is outside the country they belong to or normally reside in
- Is unable or unwilling to return home for fear of persecution.

Source: Refugee Council of Great Britain

An **asylum seeker** is someone who is waiting for their application to be recognised as a refugee to be considered by the Government.

FACT OR FICTION?

There has been so much negative media attention surrounding immigration that knowing where fact ends and fiction begins can be difficult. Try the quiz below; then read on to find out the facts.

QUIZ

Answer the following questions (true or false):

1. Asylum-seekers and refugees do not make a positive contribution to this country
2. Britain should not offer safe haven to people fleeing war or persecution
3. Only a few asylum-seekers in this country are genuine.

Answers

1. False. A Home Office report estimates that foreign-born people – including refugees and asylum seekers – contribute £2.5 billion a year to the government. See the 'Scroungers or providers' section below for more information on how refugees contribute.
2. False. The UK has a legal obligation to allow people to seek asylum – see the 'Law' section below for more information on this.
3. False. In fact close to a half are recognised as having legitimate grounds to remain in the UK.

(Quiz based on a MORI poll, 'Refugee Week 2003: A Survey of 15–24-year-olds', commissioned by Amnesty International UK, Refugee Action and the Refugee Council.)

THE LAW

The law relating to the rights of refugees was made after World War II, when there were millions of refugees in Europe. It is known as the 1951 United Nations Convention Relating to the Status of Refugees ('The Refugee Convention'). At the time, it only applied to refugees in and from Europe – but in 1967, it was extended to apply to the whole world – the 'UN Protocol Relating to the Status of Refugees' meant that the Refugee Convention rules could be applied to any person, anywhere in the world, at any time.

The United Kingdom, along with over 130 other countries, is a signatory to the Convention and/or the Protocol. That means it has a legal duty to care for refugees.

SCROUNGERS OR PROVIDERS?

A common stereotype is that refugees come into this country with the intention of claiming the dole rather than working. But a report called 'Paying their Way' by the Institute for Public Policy Research (IPPR) has revealed that immigrants are paying more into the public purse than their UK-born counterparts. The report found:

■ Total money received from immigrants grew in real terms from £33.8 billion in 1999–2000 to £41.2 billion in 2003–04 (this is a 22% increase, compared to a 6% increase for the UK-born).
■ Immigrants made up 8.7% of the population but paid 10.2% of all income tax collected (2003–2004).
■ Immigrants earn about 15% more in average weekly income than UK-born.

- Each immigrant generated on average £7203 in income for the government in 2003–2004, compared to £6861 per non-immigrant.
- On average the government spent £7277 on each immigrant, compared to £7753 per non-immigrant.

The Council for Assisting Refugee Academics estimates that there are 1500 doctors, dentists and other health workers living as refugees in Britain, but that only a few are employed as such. A further 2000 refugees are highly skilled in engineering, science, education, healthcare and computing, but are not being employed to the same level as they were in their countries of origin.

What's it like to be a refugee?

If you are a refugee or an asylum-seeker it can be daunting to have to adapt to a completely new and different way of life. You might have to learn a new language, find a new home, make friends and come to grips with a totally new culture. It's certainly not easy. And on top of that, you may be dealing with the negative attitudes of those around you – many refugees escape war in their own country only to be bullied and discriminated against in Britain.

CASE STUDIES

Adam's experience

Adam is in his twenties and left Zimbabwe three years ago, fleeing persecution from the government in charge. He says he didn't want to leave his family and friends and come to a strange land where he knew nobody and had nothing.

'A white friend of mine also came to settle here, but it's easier for him. He doesn't get treated like dirt. I think it's because he is white and not black.'

Nazir's experience *(courtesy of Refugee Action)*
'I found a job in a factory. When they found out I was a refugee, no one would sit next to me in the canteen.'

Immigration

Immigration is rich territory for people with prejudices. References to an 'invasion' and comments like 'they don't know their place' are still often used by people who feel their way of life and cultural values are threatened by immigrants. As explained above, some people think refugees are 'scroungers' and are keen to stir up negative images of them.

The UK is not the only country where immigration is a controversial issue; the rioting in France in late 2005 (where unrest spread from Paris to other parts of the country) shows how high racial tensions focused around the subject of migrant communities may run.

There has always been a lot of debate about immigrants coming to this country, and discussing immigration does not make you prejudiced. It is very important to recognise that there is a difference between having an interesting, thought-provoking conversation about the social and political effects of a certain issue, such as immigration, and dealing in negative generalisations that don't help anyone. Think about the difference between the two statements below. Which one is displaying prejudice?

■ If we have too much immigration, there may not be enough jobs to go round and unemployment could rise

■ Immigrants are lazy scroungers who just want to steal our jobs.

DEALING WITH RACISM

General advice on coping with prejudice and discrimination is given in Chapter 9 of this book. However, here are a few tips which are particularly relevant to racism.

Letting people know

If you are being physically attacked, confronting your attacker could be dangerous – but there are still things you can do. Report any racist attacks or comments to your parents and teachers and, if the racism is more serious, report it to the police.

Role models

There are plenty of examples of people from minority ethnic groups who have made an amazing success of their lives. Try to use them as an example to inspire you and to prove that prejudice can be overcome. Here are a few examples:

- **Music**: Craig David, Beverley Knight, Talvin Singh, Mis-Teeq
- **Film**: Halle Berry, Morgan Freeman, Will Smith, Denzel Washington
- **Television**: Lenny Henry, Konnie Huq, June Sarpong, Meera Syal, Trevor McDonald, Ian Wright, Reggie Yates
- **Sport**: Rio Ferdinand, Ashia Hansen, Audley Harrison, Emile Heskey, Kelly Holmes, Nasser Hussain, Amir Khan, Denise Lewis
- **Politics**: Diane Abbot MP, Adam Afriyie MP, Lord Desai, Shahid Malik MP.

Help is at hand

Talking about your experience with friends and/or elders can be especially helpful. Your friends may offer advice about coping and your elders, who may well have been through a similar experience, should understand what you are going through. Just talking about it might make you feel relieved and less alone.

And there are also organisations and helplines that can offer you advice and support, including some which are particularly targetted at those suffering from racist abuse, including:

- **Britkid** – website following a group of young people from different races, religions and backgrounds
- **European-wide Action Week against Racism** – helps make people more aware of the problem of racism and shows that it is unacceptable
- **Kick it out** – works through football to challenge racism
- **Leeds Racial Harassment Project** – encourages the empowerment of people of all ages to challenge racial prejudice
- **Muslim Council of Britain** – promotes co-operation, consensus and unity on Muslim affairs in the UK
- **Refugee Council** – offers support and advice to asylum seekers and refugees
- **Show Racism the Red Card** – uses famous footballers and managers to underline the fact that racism is unacceptable.

Further details on all these organisations can be found in the Helpful Organisations section at the end of this book.

Remember, it is never right to be judged on your religion or culture. You are not in the wrong and it's not your fault. And remember also that there is always hope, no matter how bad it seems. Marc Lorenzi is a Youth Worker for Leeds Racial Harrassment project and he has seen young people overcome incredible challenges: 'Quite often I feel admiration and respect for the dignity that the young subjects face their problems with … I have supported a young woman who had been subject to a number of very violent attacks both at school and in the community and constant degrading and harassment by teachers, who overcame the odds to achieve GCSE results beyond her expectations.'

HOMOPHOBIA
What is homophobia and how can you cope with it?

WHAT IS HOMOPHOBIA?

Homophobia literally means fear or hatred of homosexual (ie lesbian, gay or bisexual) people. As with other types of prejudice, fear and ignorance can lead to discriminatory behaviour.

Your experience of being lesbian, gay or bisexual will vary depending on your situation – you might feel very supported by friends, family and school, or you might face a very tough time because these people turn out to be prejudiced against your sexuality.

BACKGROUND

Life for gay people can be difficult. The statistics are not encouraging – according to Professor Ian Rivers of Queen Margaret University College, Edinburgh, about one in three lesbian, gay and bisexual young people is bullied. Nearly a third of them carry out self-harm, and nearly a fifth display symptoms associated with post-traumatic stress disorder. Common experiences include name-calling, and school can be a very difficult place to be.

Life at school

If you are gay, lesbian or bisexual, being discriminated against –
whether physically or verbally – can make life at school very difficult. In
one survey (*Bullying – Don't Suffer in Silence*, DfES, 2002), eight out
of ten school teachers at secondary schools said they were aware of
verbal homophobic bullying and one in four teachers was aware of
physical homophobic bullying.

FACT BOX

*Three out of four lesbian, gay and
bisexual adults said they had
regularly truanted from school
because of homophobic harassment
and half of them had contemplated
suicide or harming themselves
because of this prejudice.*

**Source: *Social Exclusion, Absenteeism
and Sexual Minority Youth*, I Rivers, 2000**

Research has shown that gay teenagers are more likely to under-
achieve and to play truant. This isn't surprising: after all, how can you
concentrate on schoolwork when people around you are making fun of
you or beating you up? However, playing truant is not really a solution
– the section on Dealing with homophobia later in this chapter offers
some useful alternative ways of coping.

According to Kidscape, many lesbian, gay and bisexual pupils said
bullying had affected their plans for further education and that they
were scared the bullying would continue if they went on to college.

FACT BOX

Research carried out in 2003 found that one in two gay men and one in three lesbians reported being bullied physically at school.

Source: *Mental Health and Social Wellbeing of Gay Men, Lesbians and Bisexuals in England and Wales*, Royal Free College and University College Medical School, 2003

Coming out

It's normal for most teenagers not to be sure whether they're straight or lesbian/gay. You really can't tell for certain until you've got through adolescence. If you're reading this, and you're not sure, the only important thing to remember is: it doesn't matter either way. They're equally good things to be. Don't let anyone tell you different.

Once you know for sure that you are lesbian, gay or bisexual, the next stage is to tell your family and friends – and this can be particularly challenging because not only are you coming to terms with your own sexuality, but also those around you may be making you feel bad about yourself. So how can you tell somebody, if you are being made to feel that what you are is wrong or bad? Remember, there's nothing wrong with being lesbian or gay: it's perfectly normal: millions of young people – and grown-ups – are gay and lesbian.

HOW TO TELL PEOPLE

While some parents will feel quite comfortable talking about your sexuality and be able to cope with your news, some may feel shocked, sad or angry when confronted with the fact. Maybe you've had several years to gradually come to terms with the fact that you are lesbian or gay. Your parents, when you tell them, will have had no time at all. They might also feel shut out and find it hard to accept that there is a side to you that they never knew about.

There is no single right or wrong way of coming out. However, it is worth planning it in order to make it easier both for you and for the people you are telling. Think about the following points:

- Consider your timing and the environment – you may feel that there is never an 'easy' time or place, but there are certainly bad times and contexts that you should try to avoid
- Write down your thoughts on paper to help you remember everything you want to say
- Make sure you are calm and collected
- Emphasise that you are still the same person. You still love your parents, and it is a measure of your love that you have been able to tell them about yourself after such a difficult time
- Try to think about your news from their point of view
- Try and have answers to many of the questions they may have for you.

You should be prepared for the possibility that your announcement might result in a negative reaction. Prejudice among those who care for us is not so unusual, so try to be patient and not to give way to anger if your news results in a hurtful response.

CASE STUDIES

Holly's story

'I decided to come out when I was in year eight at school. It took me about three months to build up the courage to tell anyone as I had heard of people being bullied, assaulted and even killed because of their sexuality but I felt I had to in order to live a normal life.

'I came out to my best friend first and she said she had already thought so anyway and she didn't mind. So I felt great and I thought that everyone else would be fine about it.

'But I couldn't have been more wrong. People close to me were fine as they, knowing me better than others, had already guessed – but other people in my school who found out were nasty, calling me all the names they could think of and saying they were going to beat me up because they thought I was "disgusting".

'I hated it and started to truant from school and pretend to be ill to get away from it. I regretted my decision to come out – but things started to calm down, until I started a relationship with my current partner that caused everything to flare up again. I was coming out of the girls' toilets when a group who had been giving me grief for ages started shouting things at me. I had had enough and turned to tell them to leave me alone. But one of the girls then punched me in the face.

'I felt I finally had to report it to the teachers, but the school didn't seem to sort out the problem completely so I had no choice but to report what had been happening to the police. I still get trouble from people in my town but my family as well as the lesbian and gay liaison officers I was put in touch with when I first reported what was happening to the police are helping me and my partner to have a slightly easier time.'

Michael's story
'I came out to friends in school about a year and a half ago. It was between a few good friends and me but of course the whole school knew within a couple of days. The hassle I received was intolerable, to say the least. I was sent to the school counsellor to talk about my

problems. I developed and still suffer from severe insomnia, for which I was referred to a psychiatrist, and was put on anti-depressants.

'The bullying did ease off eventually, but it has never completely gone. It's not as intense now, but it always resurfaces. I can't honestly recall a single day in which I haven't had some sort of reference to my sexuality, or some form of negative view. I'm at a loss to know how every young person in the town seems to know about me.

'My boyfriend's been much luckier than me. He rarely got as much verbal abuse and he's never suffered physical abuse.'

DEALING WITH HOMOPHOBIA

Trying to get others to be more tolerant is not an easy task. It takes time and determination – but remember, as people get to know you for who you really are, their negative views about your sexuality will begin to fade. Also, remember that, even though there is a lot of homophobia about, there are also a lot of positive attitudes, and things are gradually changing: people's attitudes have come a long way – and things are continuing to improve (as illustrated by the fact that, as of December 2005, gay couples may form civil partnerships).

'As people get to know you for who you really are, their negative views about your sexuality will begin to fade.'

General advice on coping with prejudice and discrimination is given in Chapter 9 of this book. However, here are a few tips which are particularly relevant to homophobia.

Role models

Will Young is a great role model: he won *Pop Idol*, and announced he was gay in 2002; his first record went on to become the fastest-selling debut single in UK history. He is successful, and he is proud to be gay. In an interview with the *News of the World*, the former drama student said: 'I feel it's time to tell my fans I'm gay. It's totally no big deal, just part of who I am. For me it's normal and nothing to be ashamed about. I'm gay and I'm comfortable with that. I really don't know what the fuss is about.'

And there are plenty of other gay icons – for example, Ellen DeGeneres, Stephen Fry, Stephen Gately, Boy George, kd lang, George Michael, Graham Norton and Michael Stipe.

Help is at hand

Your teachers, family and friends may all want to help. Even if they haven't faced the same prejudices you do, they may understand some of the feelings you have and be able to offer you advice and tips for coping, especially at school.

There are always people on your side – even if your family or classmates do not seem to be. For example, as homosexuality becomes more talked about, schools are keen to understand how they can help you. They are being encouraged to talk about homophobia in the classroom, to get rid of abusive graffiti from school walls and to encourage gay staff, governors and parents into the school environment. This can make a huge difference – as Sarah knows: 'Finally at 16 I had a teacher I knew to be gay. She was widely respected at my school and everyone wanted to be in her class. Her influence made a huge difference to my self-confidence after years of homophobic bullying.' So although you might feel alone at school, you can be sure that work is being done to tackle the prejudice you face.

There are organisations and support groups that tackle homophobia – a list of these is given in the Helpful Organisations section at the end of this book. You could also ask for a gay liaison officer to help. These officers can provide you, your family and your friends with support and help you deal with homophobic incidents. Your local police station should be able to put you in touch with a gay liaison officer.

There are people out there who will know what you are going through – people who will listen to you and give you some of the answers you need. You are not alone.

CHAPTER SIX:

DISABILITY
Dealing with discrimination if you have a disability

Prejudice is a big issue if you have a disability, and it could be that you get a taste of discrimination every time you leave your house. This chapter looks at how people respond to those with disabilities and offers some ways of coping.

HOW DO PEOPLE SHOW THEIR PREJUDICES ABOUT THOSE WITH DISABILITIES?

You might feel that people without a disability don't really make an effort to find out what life is like for you. You might find that they rely on preconceived ideas or stereotypical views about disability – as Jared did when he did a survey as part of one of his A level courses: 'I remember doing a disability survey for my A levels where I asked, "What's the first thing that comes into your head upon hearing the word 'disabled'?". Over 90% of those surveyed said a wheelchair when only 2% of disabled people use wheelchairs.'

Fourteen-year-old Tom, who has rheumatoid arthritis, comments that 'People don't know how to talk to me. I think it's because they're ignorant about my condition.' Sometimes people just don't seem to know how to act around you – as 16-year-old Sarah explains: 'Some people around me don't cope very well with people in wheelchairs and I feel like shouting "Hello! I am here, you know!" I hate it when they don't involve me in their conversations because they are standing up chatting away over my head. It can feel very lonely.' Some people over-compensate for their feelings of awkwardness or superiority, making far too much effort to be nice and consequently behaving in a patronising or condescending manner.

> 'People don't know how to talk to me. I think it's because they're ignorant about my condition.'
>
> **Tom**

But it's not just individuals who are responsible for discriminating against you. Institutions (like schools, shops, museums or workplaces) can be equally discriminatory by, for example, not providing you with adequate access – and that doesn't just mean ramps for wheelchair users; it means textphones or induction loops for those with hearing difficulties or braille versions of resources – and a whole host of other things. And think about transport companies – is it easy getting a bus or a train? Prejudice can come from every area of life and you'll know if it's affecting you when you begin to wonder if you have the same rights and privileges as a non-disabled person. (You should not be in any doubt about this – you do. In fact the law has recently been amended to make sure that it fully protects disabled people – see page 52 for more information on this.)

Are some disabilities subject to greater prejudice than others?

If your disability is very obvious, it's more likely to provoke a greater degree of prejudice. Some people react more negatively towards someone if their disability is visible. On the other hand, if your disability is obvious, you might find others are more likely to make changes to suit you and to try and be more helpful.

Non-visible disabilities, such as cerebral palsy for example, don't attract as much negative attention but can cause misunderstandings and misconceptions.

BACKGROUND

In 2002, the charity Whizz-Kidz commissioned a survey, 'People Like Us', of young able-bodied and disabled people. Their findings revealed how little contact and interaction there is between young able-bodied and disabled people:

- Two-thirds of the young physically disabled people interviewed had experienced prejudice because of their disability.
- Two-thirds of the young able-bodied people interviewed had never spoken to a physically disabled person of their own age.
- Over half believed that their disabled peers are more likely to be bullied and 'treated like freaks'.

The survey concluded that any negative attitudes or views were dramatically reduced if there was a friendship between a young able-bodied and a young disabled person – and that is starting to happen. Since the Disability Discrimination Act has been passed (under which mainstream schools must now accept disabled pupils), able-bodied pupils are mixing with disabled students, and that's a step towards both spending more time together, dispelling myths, improving attitudes and – hopefully – teaching tolerance. For more information on the law, see page 52.

The media

The media has a very strong influence on people's opinions, as explained in Chapter 2 of this book. Think about how many disabled teenagers or adults you see on TV. Newsreaders? Characters in soap operas? Pop singers? It's more than likely you can count on the fingers of one hand the number of famous disabled people you see frequently in the media – and research has shown that this plays a part in the negative reactions of the general public towards disabled people. In 2003, six disabled teenagers carried out a survey, 'Disability on the Box'. With the help of Whizz-Kidz, they found that:

- Seven out of ten of those questioned thought that able-bodied people's attitudes towards disabled people would improve if they regularly saw disabled people on TV.
- Almost two-thirds thought the best way of encouraging able-bodied people to see disabled people as 'normal' was to watch them on mainstream TV programmes where there is no focus on their disability.
- For two-thirds of young disabled people, seeing disabled role models on TV had a positive effect, inspiring them and making them hopeful that negative attitudes towards disabled people will change in the future.
- Eight out of ten people could not recall any TV advertisements that featured disabled people and three-quarters thought advertisers left disabled people out of advertisements.

The pressures of growing up

Jared O'Mara from the British Council of Disabled People comments that 'Prejudice is a given for every disabled person. Every disabled person I've talked to – and myself included – has endured traumatic teenage years. It's enough for any young person to have to deal with the pressures of growing up and raging hormones, but when you add the pressure of having a disability – in a world not made for disabled people – on top of that, it becomes awful.' For example, even though you may not find it difficult to make friends, you might find it almost impossible to imagine ever having a boyfriend or a girlfriend – and this can cause a great deal of anxiety and lead to low self-esteem.

DEALING WITH PREJUDICE AGAINST DISABILITY

General advice on coping with prejudice and discrimination is given in Chapter 9 of this book. However, here are a few tips which are particularly relevant to those with disabilities.

You should always remember that no one has the right to subject you to prejudice and discrimination. Start by believing in yourself, and others will believe in you too. In the words of Rachel Hurst of Disabled People's International: 'Social change initially comes from us, from disabled people. It has to.'

Opening minds

You may ask why it's down to you to make the effort to change other people's attitudes. Shouldn't they be making the effort? Of course they should – but you can help them. Sometimes people are unsure about how to relate to disabled people. They don't want to say or do the wrong thing or offend you. So you must be comfortable with yourself and show you can take control of the situation. Send a signal to others that they can be comfortable too.

You may also find that people want to help you do things in order to protect you. So it's up to you to make sure that they see what you are capable of. Be open and vocal about your feelings and how you would like to be treated. That way, people can begin to understand where support ends and over-protectiveness begins, for you.

Look at what you bring to society and take every opportunity to promote it. Be positive, flexible, adaptable, creative and patient – your attitude will open many doors. Above all, don't allow others to discourage you. Follow your dreams and don't be too proud to ask for help when you need it.

> *'Be open and vocal about your feelings and how you would like to be treated.'*

Role models

The Whizz-Kidz survey mentioned earlier in this chapter showed how helpful positive role models can be – and luckily there are plenty around to inspire you. For example, Tanni Grey Thompson, who was born with spina bifida and is paralysed from the waist down. Her first big achievement came when she represented Wales in the Junior National Games aged 15. Her massive trophy haul now includes 11 Paralympic gold medals after victories in the T53 100m and T53 400m in Athens in 2004. She was named a Dame in the New Year's Honours List, adding to her MBE in 1993 and the OBE she was awarded in 1999.

Another good role model is the artist Alison Lapper, who was born with no arms or legs as the result of a condition called phocomelia. Her mother didn't want to take care of her so Alison grew up in a care home. Since then, her talents and ambition have made her famous. She's a recognised artist with an MBE and a statue of her can be seen in Trafalgar Square. And there are plenty more examples of disabled people who are incredibly successful – just think of the musician Evelyn Glennie or the Politician David Blunkett. Looking at the achievements of people with disabilities should make you realise that you are as able as anyone else.

The law

The Disability Discrimination Act (DDA) 1995 aimed to end the discrimination which many disabled people face. It ensured that disabled people have rights in the areas of:

- Employment
- Education
- Access to goods, facilities and services
- Buying or renting land or property.

The Act also allowed the government to set minimum standards that would enable disabled people to use public transport easily. The DDA 1995 has now been amended and extended by the new Disability Discrimination Act 2005 (DDA 2005), which:

- Makes it unlawful for operators of transport vehicles to discriminate against disabled people
- Makes it easier for disabled people to rent property and for tenants to make disability-related adaptations
- Makes sure that private clubs with 25 or more members cannot keep disabled people out, just because they have a disability
- Extends protection to cover people who have HIV infection, cancer and multiple sclerosis from the moment they are diagnosed
- Ensures that discrimination law covers all the activities of the public sector
- Requires public bodies to promote equality of opportunity for disabled people.

Some of the new laws came into force in December 2005, and some will come into force in December 2006. Changing the way people think and act takes a long time, and there is no easy fix to the problems that you might be facing – but the law is there to protect your rights. The Disability Rights Commission (DRC) website has more details.

Help is at hand

There are many organisations willing to help see you through the difficulties and trauma of prejudice. Of course, there are also friends and family who will take the time to listen to you. And if a fellow disabled person is on hand to listen, you should have no problems or inhibitions in opening up. Just sharing your experiences with someone else who may have gone through something similar has the power to go a long way in the healing process.

Once you find the best coping mechanisms for you, your experiences will undoubtedly become more positive. For Jared, discovering methods of coping meant that he rarely looks back.

CASE STUDY

Jared's story

'I spent my entire teenage years secretly depressed and had no one to turn to. Despite my disability I was always bright, funny and immensely popular and was fortunate enough to have a plethora of amazing friends. I gave out an air of confidence and indifference to the negative side of my disability in order to avoid the fact that I was actually messed up inside.

'Being bullied was commonplace, whether it is through name-calling (I still will not tolerate the word "spaz") or physical. When I got to about the age of ten, rather than just accept it, I learnt to fight back.

And at secondary school, despite having mild cerebral palsy, I became a bit of a bad lad and was no stranger to fighting (and winning) as well as being disobedient, irreverent and truant. And as bad as it sounds, it gained me the respect and admiration of my peers.

'At sixth form I reached my nadir. I was no longer a bad lad, though I still played truant – even more so than usual – and I was really into my A levels, enjoying them in the main. However, I was the most insecure I'd ever been about my disability and, as I was at an entirely new school to the one I took my GCSEs at, I became sullen, withdrawn and self-loathing. Also, when you're 16–18 most of your peers are embarking on serious relationships with members of the opposite sex. Though I wanted this dearly I was convinced no girl would want me because of my disability.

'When I got to university, this mindset continued, but it gradually got better and by the time I was in my third year a complete metamorphosis had occurred. I was now confident, passionate and driven. I graduated with a First and even lectured one third-year module, even though I was an undergraduate like everyone else.

'Twelve months later I applied this new-found confidence and passion and became the youngest disabled person ever to stand for election – in the city council elections in Sheffield. I am also heavily involved in music and the music industry, as a manager, scout, promoter and occasional nightclub DJ.

'The change in me occurred because I wanted it to. The glass is either half empty or half full and only you can decide which.'

CHAPTER SEVEN

LEARNING AND COMMUNICATION DIFFERENCES

How people respond to conditions like autism, Asperger's syndrome or dyslexia, and how to cope

We are all different. We all look different and we all have varying physical abilities. But there are some differences that aren't so obvious. For example, we have all had different experiences based on our culture and religion. And we all have different mental abilities – for example, the way we learn or communicate may be different from the way some of our classmates learn.

INVISIBLE DIFFERENCES

Those with learning and communication differences are not visibly disabled in the same way someone who is blind or who has cerebral palsy may be. Because of this, it can be very difficult to create an awareness and understanding of your condition, and your symptoms

'Because you might be physically the same as they are, people might expect you to behave the same way as they do.'

can be mistaken for being slow, stupid or naughty. This is not the case at all. It's simply about your brain working in a different way.

Living with a learning or communication difference can be a very lonely experience. People may often discriminate against you because they don't understand anything about your condition: and because you might be physically the same as they are, they might expect you to behave the same way as they do.

Lack of understanding and bullying are particularly common forms of discrimination against those with learning and communication differences.

This may be because your condition makes you behave differently in certain situations, and also makes you less able to defend yourself or to communicate what has happened.

This chapter will look in detail at some of the more common learning and communication differences, and outline ways of coping with the effects of the discrimination you may experience.

AUTISM AND ASPERGER'S SYNDROME

What is autism?

The National Autistic Society defines autism as follows: 'Autism is a lifelong developmental disability that affects the way a person communicates and relates to people around them. Children and adults with autism have difficulties with everyday communication and the way they socialise. Their ability to develop friendships is generally limited as is their capacity to understand other people's emotional expression.' People with autism generally experience three main areas of difficulty:

- **Social interaction** – difficulty with social relationships, for example appearing laid-back, not interested in or indifferent to other people
- **Social communication** – difficulty with verbal and non-verbal communication, for example not fully understanding the meaning of common gestures (a handshake, for instance), facial expressions or tone of voice
- **Imagination** – difficulty in the development of interpersonal play and imagination, for example having a limited range of imaginative activities, possibly copied and pursued rigidly and repetitively.

In addition to these difficulties, repetitive behaviour patterns and resistance to change in routine are often characteristic in people with autism too.

Fast facts on autism

- There are approximately 535,000 people with autism in the UK.
- Boys are four times more likely to develop autism than girls.
- 21% of children with an autistic spectrum disorder have been excluded from school at least once.
- People with autism often want to make friends but find it difficult because of their condition.

Source: The National Autistic Society

Living with autism

Perhaps the most difficult part of coping with autism is interacting with other people every day. Because the brain of a teenager with autism works a little differently, learning to communicate can be like learning a foreign language.

This can make it hard for you to express yourself or for other people to understand you, so just talking with a classmate becomes stressful and frustrating.

CASE STUDY

Janet's Story

'At primary school, I found playtime to be excruciating, never being able to work out what was going on in tag games for example, and preferred to stay safe, with my back against the wall. Teachers would have to cajole me to play with the others, but I would creep back to my wall refuge as soon as their backs were turned. To make matters worse, I could not catch a ball if it was thrown in my direction, so no one wanted me to take part in their games. I never, ever get the hang of teasing and sarcasm and always take everything literally. Some people found this cute but I regard teasing as abject cruelty.'

Courtesy of The National Autistic Society

When even a casual conversation requires so much effort, it's obviously hard to make friends. And then there's the additional anxiety about what your classmates will think of you. Living with autism means you have to think constantly about how other people will perceive your actions and make a conscious effort to pay attention to social cues that those without autism can handle without even thinking. It takes a lot of work for a person with autism to do what comes naturally to most people.

What is Asperger's syndrome?

Asperger's syndrome is a mild form of autism and it shares many of the same characteristics. Many people with Asperger's have difficulty in understanding how others think and feel. This may lead to naive or socially inappropriate behaviour.

Living with Asperger's syndrome

Teenagers with Asperger's try hard to be sociable but they can find it difficult to understand non-verbal signals, including facial expressions. They may speak very fluently but they may not take any notice of the reaction of those listening to them. They might continue to talk about one topic regardless of the interest or lack of it.

Their voice and facial expression might be flat or unusual and they may have odd gestures or eye contact. In many cases they may take jokes or expressions literally and have difficulty in understanding sarcasm.

Living with Asperger's syndrome can feel very lonely. Even the thought of explaining your differences to someone else can seem daunting – as Suz explains in the case study below.

CASE STUDY

Suz's story

'I was 17 before it started to occur to me that there was just something about the way I was. I started referring to myself then as socially disabled. I tried to explain to other people that I was just different and couldn't help it, but no one took me seriously. It was eight years later I discovered Asperger's syndrome and was diagnosed. I would never have guessed. I thought I was the only one.

'I hardly ever know what to say in social situations. It is like there is just nothing in my head ... no words and no motivation, just thoughts.

When I was a kid I would imagine I was presenting a television show in order to practise speaking my thoughts. I used to say them out loud all the time back then. I would be walking home form school chatting to my imaginary viewers about my day. I didn't realise people didn't like it or that I wasn't supposed to. Years later I was told that parents told their children to stay away from me because I was always talking to myself.

'The worst part is not wanting other people to know. People find it hard to understand. Every time people ask me what I did at the weekend I feel panic, not because I didn't enjoy my weekend but because I never have anything to say ... I don't know what to say, I mean, should I lie? Should I just make something up so I sound "normal"? A person could start to live in dread of Mondays.

'These days I just tell the truth and make no secret of the fact that I don't get out much, but people look so horrified and upset, especially when it is week after week after week. I know they are probably just concerned, and that is when the advice starts ... "Why don't you go there, do that, join the other ... ? Get out and make some friends." Then what am I supposed to say? How can you explain to people that unlike them, no matter how much effort you put in, those sorts of things never work out.'

Dealing with prejudice against autism and Asperger's syndrome

General advice on coping with prejudice and discrimination is given in Chapter 9 of this book. However, here are a few tips which are particularly relevant to those with autism and Asperger's syndrome.

LETTING OTHERS GET TO KNOW YOU

Trying to work out a way forward might seem really hard. But the best way of opening up people's minds is to educate them about your condition and to show them who you are – if you can do this, there's a good chance they will become more tolerant and understanding.

GETTING TO KNOW YOURSELF

You might find it particularly hard to convey your feelings about those who are discriminating against you if you are autistic. But changes in your behaviour might reveal the signs that something is not right. For example:

■ Are you more anxious?
■ Do you feel like eating less?
■ Do you feel angry and confused?

If you notice these symptoms, try to explain to others what they show, so that they become more sensitive to the changes in your behaviour and what these might indicate.

SPECIALIST EDUCATION

Specialist education and structured support can really make a difference too, helping you to maximise your skills. Music therapy, counselling and the use of symbols can also be useful in dealing with autism. Everyone is different, so some people will find certain therapies more useful than others.

HELP IS AT HAND

Although prejudice against your condition can make you feel low and alone, remember – you don't have to deal with it by yourself. Taking time to talk things through with others who've shared the same experiences as you and also getting in touch with organisations that are used to dealing with the problems you face might be a great way to start dealing with the prejudices you face.

At the end of this book you will find a list of organisations which can offer advice, information and support. They can work through solutions with you to help manage the situation.

DYSLEXIA

What is dyslexia?

Dyslexia is a type of learning difference rather than a learning disability.

Dyslexia is the term used when people have difficulty learning to read, even though they are smart enough and are motivated to learn. A person with dyslexia has trouble processing or understanding words or numbers. Dyslexic people hear and see normally but have difficulty remembering and processing what they hear and see.

FACT BOX

It was only about 100 years ago that doctors first identified the set of learning problems that we call dyslexia. The word 'dyslexia' itself comes from two Greek words: dys, which means abnormal or impaired, and lexis, which refers to language or words.

It takes a lot of time for a person with dyslexia to sound out a word, so the meaning of the word is often lost and reading comprehension is poor. It is not surprising that some people with dyslexia also have trouble spelling, expressing themselves in writing, and even speaking because they still need to put phonemes (units of sound) together to form words, whether spoken, written, or read.

Some people with milder forms of dyslexia may have less difficulty in certain areas of spoken and written language. Some have found ways of working round their dyslexia – but it takes a lot of effort and extra work. Dyslexia isn't something that goes away on its own or that you will outgrow. People with dyslexia must find different ways to learn, and use those strategies all their lives.

What causes dyslexia?

Dyslexia is not a disease – it is a condition that you are born with, and it often runs in families. Researchers believe that it occurs because of the way that the brain is formed and the way that it processes the information it receives. People with dyslexia are actually wired differently. Pictures of the brain, taken with modern imaging tools, have shown that when people with dyslexia read they use different parts of the brain to people without dyslexia.

Although we know more about dyslexia today than we did a century ago, we're still a long way from completely understanding how and why it occurs.

Living with dyslexia

As well as having difficulty with reading and spelling, you might find that you confuse dates and times and it might seem really difficult to organise your life around a school timetable and complete your work on time. Throughout your school career you might:

- Have particular areas of strength, for example art or drama
- Appear bright and able, but find it hard to get your thoughts down on paper
- Act the 'class clown' so that you can disguise what you feel are your academic failings

FACT BOX

One in ten people has some form of dyslexia.

- Become withdrawn and isolated, sitting at the back and not wanting to take part
- Look glazed when people speak too quickly
- Be clumsy
- Be able to do one thing at a time very well but not remember an entire list
- Go home exhausted because you've put so much into your day's learning.

You might often get frustrated because, no matter how hard you try, you can't seem to keep up with other pupils in your class.

BEING MISUNDERSTOOD

The most common perception of teenagers with dyslexia is that they are stupid, lazy or disruptive. You might feel that you're being labelled unfairly and that you're being treated differently because of other people's preconceptions about your abilities.

This attitude is completely wrong: most people with dyslexia have average or above-average intelligence, and they work very hard to overcome their learning problems. Always remember that you have many talents that may yet have to be awakened.

Dyslexic people often say it is difficult to explain their dyslexia – and this can contribute to the feeling of being misunderstood. Here are some ways people have expressed how it feels to be dyslexic:

- 'My brain is wired differently.'
- 'It's like my computer crashing with too much information!'
- 'I know what I want to say, but I can never find the right words.'
- 'I see things from a different perspective.'
- 'I have all the right ideas, but I can't get them down on paper.'
- 'Speaking out in front of other people makes me stumble and forget what I was trying to say.'

Experiencing dyslexia

Here is how three young people have expressed their experience of dyslexia.

'Before I could write it down it swung away from my fading memory.'

William

Dyslexser
> I was born with it
> But because of it
> I got hit for it
> I cried about it
> Fought because of it
> Tried to get rid of it
> Albert Einstein had it
> Sulked about it
> Called names because of it
> I didn't like it
> Mum had enough of me because of it
> Couldn't be bothered to live with it

Do we really have to have it?
Mum thought I was lazy because of it
I thought I was crazy because of it
Punched walls because of it
Got in trouble over it
Disrupted class because of it
Walked out, away from it
Embarrassed because of it
I'm ashamed of it
I swore at teachers because of it
Just have to live with it

John Rogers and Lea Bourne,
reproduced courtesy of the British Dyslexia Association

CASE STUDY

Sarah is aged 13 and she hates reading aloud in class. She's never been a good reader, and even when she recognises the words on the page, she seems to have trouble saying them correctly. She often gets discouraged, thinking that she's not as smart as other students.

Fortunately, Sarah has discovered she has talents that others don't. She's great at dreaming up costume and scenery ideas in drama club, and she's one of the best artists in her school. Sometimes she wonders how she can do so well in some areas of her life and so poorly in others.

Dealing with prejudice against dyslexia

General advice on coping with prejudice and discrimination is given in Chapter 9 of this book. However, here are a few tips which are particularly relevant to those with dyslexia.

BEING POSITIVE

As explained above, people with dyslexia sometimes have trouble communicating what dyslexia is like. Try to be honest about everything you find difficult, but emphasise ways you have found to get around these problems, so that others can see how resourceful you are. Here are some examples:

- 'My spelling is poor, but I use a spellcheck and for an important document I ask someone to proofread.'
- 'I find a series of instructions difficult to follow but if I have time to make notes or a written list I can do the job.'
- 'I sometimes have to work harder and in a different way.'

It is important that you are able to accept the areas where you have strengths and those where you have weaknesses. Try not to worry if you cannot do a task: everyone has weaknesses. Having a positive and honest attitude will gain you much respect.

LOOKING TO THE FUTURE

Work or university might seem a lifetime away, but for many teenagers who are thinking about what they will do after leaving school, the thought of breaking down barriers and the myths that surround dyslexia all over again might seem all too daunting. But those with dyslexia shouldn't feel limited in their education and career choices – the future is bright.

Many colleges have made specific arrangements for students with dyslexia, offering them trained tutors, learning aids, and special arrangements for exams. You can become a politician, corporate executive, actor, artist, teacher – whatever you choose to be.

There are campaigns under way that are helping employers to think about their attitudes and practices towards young people with dyslexia starting work.

Employers are slowly but surely being made to see that dyslexic people can bring many good skills to an organisation (such as innovative, creative and lateral thinking, problem-solving, practical skills and excellent visual and spatial awareness) – and that the adjustments that need to be made to accommodate their condition are simple and inexpensive.

ROLE MODELS

There are plenty of successful people who have overcome the prejudices that surround dyslexia, including: Robbie Williams, Tom Cruise, Guy Ritchie, Richard Branson and Lee Ryan.

CASE STUDY

In an interview for the Observer *magazine (3 July 2005), Lee Ryan, who used to be in the boy band Blue, said he was an angry child, kicking his desk over and walking out of the class. His dyslexia went undiagnosed for a long time, and he says that, before they realised what his condition was, his teachers gave him a difficult time, thinking he was a troublemaker. Now Lee is a successful solo artist.*

Help is at hand

Although dealing with the prejudice surrounding dyslexia can be tough, help is available and you should not feel alone. Family and friends can help you by understanding that you aren't stupid or lazy and that you are trying as hard as you can. They can recognise and appreciate your strengths, whether they are in sports, drama, art, creative problem solving – or something else.

These days, teachers and schools are well aware of the symptoms of dyslexia and are equipped with the information they need to give you the right support, which could include special classes or a tutor who works one-to-one with you or being given more time to complete assignments. This can make you feel more in control of your learning.

WE ALL EXPERIENC[
PREJUDICE

*Why negative
opinions about
age and sex mea[
that prejudice is
an issue we must
all face*

In Chapter 1, we saw that everyone is capable of developing prejudiced
opinions. Similarly, it is likely that at some point in our lives we will all be
on the receiving end of prejudice or discrimination from other people –
even if we do not belong to any of the groups described so far in this
book. That is because there are two more major types of prejudice that
have not yet been mentioned: ageism and sexism.

AGEISM

Old fuddy-duddies?

You might think that you don't have any prejudices yourself, but you'd
be surprised. Get to 49 and it seems you could be 'over the hill' – at
least that's what many of us think, according to the charity Age
Concern. Andrew Edwards, BBC broadcaster and media lecturer,
explains: 'Say "pensioner" and many people think of someone living on
the breadline in a small flat with a single-bar fire reminiscing about the

'It is likely that at some point in our lives we will all be on the receiving end of prejudice or discrimination from other people.'

Second World War. In reality many older people are well-off, computer-friendly globetrotters spending their children's inheritance rather than sitting at home with a cat!'

It's interesting to note that half of all people under the age of 24 have no friends over 70, and vice versa. Without first-hand experience of the abilities and attitudes of different generations, it's all too easy to stick to our safe world of stereotypes. If we don't know anyone who is old, how can we make judgements about them? What do we base our attitudes on? We think old people are out of touch and traditional – in fact research shows they are more youthful than ever, and more adventurous in terms of hobbies and activities.

Moody teenagers?

But it's not just older people who can experience prejudice. As a teenager, you too might feel you're being stereotyped as moody and lazy. Professor Philip Graham, a psychiatrist at the London Institute of

FACT BOX

From age 55 onwards, people are nearly twice as likely to have experienced age prejudice than any other form of discrimination.

Source: Age Concern

Child Health, says teenagers are being wrongly branded as moody and troublesome. He says it's not true that they are confused about their identity and frequently argue with their parents.

FACT BOX

A BBC survey of 16,000 teenagers found many adolescents agreed they get a 'bad press', with only 13% agreeing that society values teenagers.

Almost one in five felt that this stereotyping was the hardest thing – above exam pressures and boyfriend/girlfriend relationships.

SEXISM

Just like age, sex is another common root of prejudice and lazy stereotyping. Have you ever heard the James Brown song *It's a man's, man's, man's world*? Do you agree? Your answer may depend on whether you're a girl or a boy. In fact men have been in charge for centuries – but that began to change when suffragettes like Emmeline Pankhurst campaigned for equal rights for women around the turn of the twentieth century.

A girl born in the early 1900s had little chance of doing anything else except what was expected of her: to marry young, stay at home and

FACT BOX

- *Women under the age of 30 were not allowed to vote until 1928*
- *Girls did not have an automatic right to go to school until 1944.*

raise a family (or go into domestic service). The twentieth century saw a lot of progress for girls and women. Education, politics, sport and many other arenas that were once dominated by males have now opened up to women.

But there are still barriers that face women because of their sex. There are certain jobs that are still regarded as 'male' – for example, some jobs in the financial sector, science and engineering are still regarded by some as macho and unwelcoming to women.

And men can also face discrimination because of their sex. For example, fathers have only recently been granted paternity leave. According to 2005 figures, only one in ten nurses are men, and there are only 115 practising male midwives in the UK (Nursing and

FACT BOX

- *Only two out of every ten MPs are women*
- *On average, the hourly earnings for women working full time are 18% lower than for men working full time.*

Midwifery Council). Given the shortage of nurses, there has been a positive move to encourage men into this profession, which has traditionally been regarded as a female one.

CONCLUSION

We will all be affected by ageism and sexism at some point in our lives – and this underlines the fact that prejudice is an issue that everyone needs to address. It is not something that just affects a small minority of people (those in very specific groups and those with very specific opinions) – it is something we must all face up to. The next chapter offers advice on how to cope if people are behaving in a discriminatory way towards you, and also looks at ways of making sure that the future is a more equal and less prejudiced place.

CHAPTER NINE:

OVERCOMING PREJUDICE
*Different ways
of dealing with
prejudice*

So far this book has outlined the causes and effects of prejudice, and
explored in detail some of the different types of prejudice that exist.
The final part of this book will offer you ideas and advice on how to
cope if – for whatever reason – people's behaviour towards you is
demonstrating discrimination and prejudice. The first section, 'Coping
with prejudice', offers ways of coping with the short-term effects of
discrimination, and the second section looks to the future, towards
finding ways of making sure that, eventually, prejudice is stamped out
once and for all.

COPING WITH PREJUDICE

Coping with prejudice is not easy – it takes confidence as well as time.
However, there are plenty of ways you can keep up your morale – and
there are people you can turn to for support if it all gets too much.

Helping yourself

IT'S NOT YOUR FAULT

The first, and most important, way of coping with other people's
prejudice is to remember that **it is never your fault**. It never was, it

never will be, and nothing you will ever do could mean that you deserve it. You haven't done anything wrong. Keep asking yourself what's wrong with those who are prejudiced, rather than asking yourself what is wrong with you.

YOU ARE NOT ALONE

You'd be surprised at how many people around you have been touched by discrimination – your parents or carers, the shopkeeper on the high street, a teacher or even the person who is discriminating against you – many of us have experienced prejudice at one time or another. This should mean that there are plenty of people who you can talk to – for more on this, see the section below on 'Asking others for support'.

TAKING YOUR TIME AND STAYING CALM

Don't put yourself under pressure by thinking you have to bounce back quickly or always be happy. Learning to deal with prejudice takes time. There is no easy answer, no quick fix, and much of it is about changing the way people and institutions think (see 'Stopping the vicious circle of prejudice', below) – so cut yourself some slack and be gentle with yourself.

Try to stay calm. If you feel threatened, seek out a friendly face – a schoolmate or a teacher. If you feel unsafe, walk away. Find somewhere secure, perhaps where there are adults around. Keep a diary so that if you do need further help you can refer back to incidents that have happened before.

BEING PRACTICAL AND BEING POSITIVE

Things will be easier if you try to be as practical and realistic as possible – without letting things get you down. Try the following:

■ Be honest about the problem with yourself and your peers

■ Gather as much support as possible from as many places as you can

■ Understand that everyone can support you in different ways

■ Keep faith in the system, even if everything seems hopeless

■ Focus on where you want to be and not where you are

■ Realise that experience makes you stronger and gives you skills that you can pass on to others.

The charity Whizz-Kidz also offers a few tips to help you take control:

■ Talk to people you trust and whose opinion you respect. They might be able to advise you. And even if they can't, talking about it will help you.

■ Break the problem down into manageable parts and you may find it easier to deal with.

■ Look at the problem from another perspective – particularly that of the person you think is causing it.

■ Look through the problem – visualising the outcome you want may help you find a solution.

■ Sleep on it – problems can look very different in the morning.

■ Learn from others – very few problems are unique, and you may be able to use the experiences of others to find a solution.

Courtesy of Whizz-Kidz

REBUILDING YOUR SELF-ESTEEM

As we saw in Chapter 3, prejudice can harm your self-esteem, so recognising that you can improve the way you feel about yourself is vitally important. Here are some steps you can take to help combat any negative feelings you might have about yourself as a result of discrimination:

- Each day, write down three things about yourself that make you happy.
- Think about what you're good at and what you enjoy, and build on those abilities. Take pride in new skills you develop and talents you have. Share what you can do with others.
- Exercise! You'll relieve stress, and be healthier and happier.
- Try to stop thinking negative thoughts about yourself. When you catch yourself being too self-critical, counter it by saying something positive about yourself.
- Take pride in your opinions and ideas – and don't be afraid to voice them.
- Remember to look at your inner beauty – which is more than skin deep.
- Set goals. Think about what you'd like to accomplish; then make a plan for how to do it. Stick with your plan and keep track of your progress.
- Make a contribution. Tutor a classmate who's having trouble, help clean up your neighbourhood, take part in an event for a good cause. Feeling that you're making a difference can do wonders to improve self-esteem.
- Have fun – enjoy spending time with the people you care about and doing the things you love.

EXPRESSING YOUR FEELINGS

Experiencing prejudice can make you feel upset, angry, frustrated, depressed … It is important that you do not keep these feelings to yourself. The most important thing to do is make sure you talk to someone about them (see below), but you might also find other ways

Writing down your thoughts, talking about your experiences and developing your talents to express how you feel can be great ways of letting out your anger, confusion and feelings of hurt.

of expressing them – for example by getting involved in creative activities such as music, pottery, poetry, photography or drama. This can help you get to know people as well as developing your own creative skills.

LETTING PEOPLE KNOW WHO YOU ARE

As we saw in the first chapter, prejudices are based on stereotypes about groups of people in general, which ignore individual differences and personalities. Once people learn about you they will begin to feel less scared. In reality, the person who is causing you trouble may be pretty nice deep down – it's just that they haven't learned about the differences between you and them. So they need help too.

Trying to get people to know you for who you are rather than on the basis of wrong information is an important step towards overcoming prejudice. Think of it as educating them about what you are really like. This is not at all easy – and the thought of getting someone to change the way they think and the views they have of you might seem impossible. But prejudice can be overcome. It's a slow process and it depends on other people making the effort to challenge their own assumptions – but it can be done. The section on 'Breaking the vicious circle of prejudice', later in this chapter, outlines how the barriers built up by prejudice can gradually be broken down.

Asking others for support

Although you may not know it, there are people who want to help you: people who have experienced similar discrimination and those who've discovered different ways of getting through it. There are friends and family who might just have been through what you are going through now. There are support groups that are willing to listen to you – many of these are listed in the Helpful Organisations section at the end of this book.

If you feel you can't go on and none of the tips offered so far in this chapter seem to make any difference, you must seek help. If you don't feel able to talk to your family, friends or teachers, then you can contact one of the helplines listed in the Helpful Organisations section at the end of this book. Talking about it can help a lot.

COUNSELLING

Also on your side are trained professionals who have lots of experience helping teenagers facing prejudice. They will listen to you and help you find a way forward. In the box below, Philip Hodson answers some frequently asked questions on counselling.

Interview with Phillip Hodson

Phillip Hodson is an agony uncle who's helped thousands of teenagers, and a Fellow of the British Association for Counselling and Psychotherapy.

How can counselling help?
'In so many ways – you can feel understood, totally accepted yourself, helped to look at the problems of those discriminating against you (possibly they are mentally unstable); you can offload your feelings, consider new strategies and gain in overall confidence.'

Will it be easy to talk to a stranger?
'Probably easier than talking to a friend or relative because you can say – literally – anything you like.'

Can I do it in confidence?
'All counselling is guaranteed to be confidential – some is secret – unless you admit to something like a murder, in which case there is a higher legal duty to report it!'

Can I bring a friend?
'Not into the session. They can wait for you in the waiting area.'

Will I have to pay?
'It depends – some counselling is voluntary and free, some is available through your GP on the NHS, and some is subsidised through youth organisations. The rest does cost – since therapists also need to eat.'

How do I go about finding a counsellor?
'Contact the British Association for Counselling and Psychotherapy – www.bacp.co.uk – you can search for a therapist by town or county. Or phone 0870 443 5243. BACP is by far the largest organisation in this field in Europe, with over 25,000 members.'

How can a stranger understand my problems?
'They can understand your difficulties because they are open to listening to you without prejudice themselves – you are not their child or other relative – they are not 'part of the problem' and they also know that many problems arise for similar reasons to do with the nature of family and society itself – they have studied and trained in the field of psychology.'

STOPPING THE VICIOUS CIRCLE OF PREJUDICE

The first part of this chapter should have given you some ideas on how you can cope with prejudice. This part of the chapter will look at some more long-term ways of breaking the cycle of prejudice. In order to stop prejudice affecting us and others in the future, we need to change people's attitudes – and we need to know how to make sure we never become prejudiced ourselves.

People who discriminate need help in understanding the differences between them and you. If they are taught to be more understanding and tolerant, their prejudiced behaviour will probably diminish.

Tolerance and respect

Tolerance means adopting an attitude of openness and respect for the differences that exist among us. It is about accepting people for who they are. It also means treating others the way you would like to be treated yourself.

Tolerance means:

- Respecting and learning from others
- Valuing differences
- Bridging cultural gaps
- Rejecting unfair stereotypes
- Discovering common ground
- Creating new bonds.

FACT BOX

Tolerance does not mean that all behaviours have to be accepted. Behaviours that disrespect or hurt others (like bullying) and behaviours that break social rules (like lying or stealing) should never be tolerated. Respect is about accepting people for who they are – but it is not about accepting bad behaviour.

Tolerance and respect are, in many ways, the opposite of prejudice and discrimination. This book has shown that we all have stereotypical views about something or other – so we can all benefit from learning how to be tolerant. Here are a few tips on making sure that you approach life with a tolerant outlook:

■ **Don't judge a person on your first impression** – which is usually based just on the way they look. Take the time to learn more about that person than what is on the surface.
■ **Keep an open mind**. It may be easier to spend time with people who seem just like you, but you can miss out on a lot of interesting experiences – conversations, food, books, music and art, sports, religious ceremonies, and more. Getting to know people who seem different can be difficult at first, but you'll probably find that you have much more in common than you think.
■ **Be informed** about what's happening in the world. Find out how you can contribute – for example, you might volunteer with a human rights organisation. If you enjoy playing music or writing, you might try using those skills to express and share your feelings.
■ **Think about how others feel**. Take a look at the exercise in the box below and try to imagine how it would feel to be different.

As we saw in Chapter 2, we all have a responsibility to challenge our own prejudices – even if they have been taught to us at a very young age.

Empathy

Try to imagine how it must feel to be someone else. You probably know lots of people who have something that sets them apart from the norm. All of these people have feelings and deserve to be accepted for who they are.

Even if you don't consider yourself to be prejudiced, it is easy to make an off-the-cuff remark (for example, to make fun of someone's accent) that you mean as a joke, but that does not feel like a joke to the person on the receiving end. Before you say anything, think how the person you are saying it to might feel.

Try reading through the text below to help you understand what it might be like to stand out from the crowd.

Imagine your parents have just told you that you are moving to Mars. You don't know anything about the clothes they wear there, the food they eat, what the schools are like, whether there are cars or whether everyone travels around in spaceships, or whether or not you'll need to learn a different language so that the Martians will be able to understand you.

The idea of going to live in a new place with aliens and spaceships might seem exciting at first. In fact, your first week on Mars is fun – it feels like a holiday. But imagine week two in your new home. You begin to feel anxious and alone. You've started missing your friends and family. They don't have the same shops on Mars. You have to eat strange food and learn a new language.

At school, the teachers don't really know very much about the country you've left behind. They wonder why you need to heat up your house with radiators, when you could just use cosmic rays. They wonder why you eat sweets when you could enjoy Martian delicacies such as roasted Jrjklknm.

Being different can feel very strange and lonely. Is it easy speaking up about your culture? Will the Martians understand? What if the teacher keeps trying to help by telling the rest of the class about where you've come from, but keeps getting it wrong? How easy will it be to explain to your classmates what your house was like on earth when they have always been told that earthlings live in tents?

Celebrating differences
No two people in the world are exactly alike. Everyone, even identical twins, has their own experiences and their own viewpoints. You don't have to like the same food, sports or music as your friends, or practise the same religion. But being open to learning about their differences makes it easier to live harmoniously and means that you are less likely to develop prejudiced opinions, because the more we learn about people, the more likely we are to realise that the myths and stereotypes we hear are unfair or incorrect.

FACT BOX

Knowing someone who is gay or lesbian reduces by half the likelihood of being prejudiced against gay or lesbian people as a group. Similarly, knowing someone from a different ethnic group reduces by half the likelihood of being prejudiced against people from different ethnic groups.
Source: Stonewall

Respecting and celebrating difference opens the door into an exciting world of diversity. You will find that everyone has something to offer, even if it's something unexpected, like a new idea or a different way of looking at something. Remember – you don't have to agree with someone to respect their right to have an opinion or to learn from them – you can respect each other's right to differ and enjoy having conversations where you find out more about their views.

Of course, celebrating others' differences doesn't mean giving up your own heritage. Your family may be proud of their own cultural and religious traditions, but they can still find ways of celebrating the differences of others while continuing to honour their own heritage and pass it on to you.

Living together harmoniously relies on tolerance. Understanding that we are all different, learning about those differences and not feeling threatened by them will help to break down prejudice.

Good luck, and remember: those people who discriminate are never right and never will be. Prejudice is wrong – full stop.

HELPFUL ORGANISATIONS

The final section in this book is a list of organisations and contacts you can go to for help. Most have confidential helplines and all have websites for you to tap into for advice and information.

GENERAL CONTACTS

Childline
Tel: 0800 1111
Web: www.childline.org.uk
Childline is a free 24-hour national helpline for young people in trouble or danger.

Connexions
Tel: 0808 001 3219
Web: www.connexions.gov.uk
Confidential advice, support and information for 13- to 19-year-olds.

Kidscape
2 Grosvenor Gardens
London SW1W 0DH
Tel: 020 7730 3300

Helpline: 08451 205204
Web: www.kidscape.org.uk
An organisation that tackles bullying and abuse.

NSPCC

Helpline: 0808 800 5000
Web: www.nspcc.org.uk
The NSPCC's mission is to end cruelty to children. Its website offers advice on a range of issues including bullying, and its helpline is available 24/7.

Samaritans

Tel: 0845 790 9090
Web: www.samaritans.org.uk
Confidential emotional support, 24 hours a day, for people experiencing feelings of distress and despair, or contemplating suicide.

RACISM

Britkid

Web: www.britkid.org
The Britkid website follows a group of young people from different races, religions and backgrounds. They talk about the different hassles they have and how they deal with them. The 'teachers' area of the website also has a useful list of publications, organisations and websites.

Commission for Racial Equality (CRE)

St Dunstan's House
201–11 Borough High Street
London SE1 1GZ
Tel: 020 7939 0000

Web: www.cre.gov.uk
Works towards the elimination of racial discrimination and promotes equality of opportunity.

European-wide Action Week against Racism

Web: www.united.non-profit.nl/pages/camparw.htm
Helps make people more aware of the problem of racism and shows that it is unacceptable.

Kick It Out

PO Box 29544
London EC2A 4WR
Tel: 020 7684 4884
Web: www.kickitout.org
The 'Let's Kick Racism Out of Football' campaign began in 1993. All of football's governing bodies, supporters' organisations and local authorities support the campaign and work to challenge racism at all levels.

Leeds Racial Harassment Project

Tel: 0113 293 5100
Web: www.lrhp.org.uk
Email: info@lrhp.org.uk
The Leeds Racial Harassment Project aims to encourage the empowerment of people of all ages to challenge racial prejudice from a position of independence.

Muslim Council of Britain

Boardman House
64 Broadway, Stratford
London E15 1NT
Tel: 020 8432 0585/6

Web: www.mcb.org.uk
Promotes co-operation, consensus and unity on Muslim affairs in the UK.

Refugee Council
Tel: 020 7820 3000
Web: www.refugeecouncil.org.uk
The Refugee Council offers support and advice to asylum seekers and refugees. It has an informative website covering the experience of refugees, the latest news and campaigns, as well as a 'press myths' section challenging the reporting of asylum issues.

Show Racism the Red Card
Show Racism the Red Card
PO Box 141, Whitley Bay
Tyne & Wear NE26 3YH
Tel: 0191 291 0160
Web: www.srtrc.org
Email: ged@theredcard.org
Uses famous footballers and managers to underline the fact that racism is unacceptable. They also provide information and educational resources if you want to promote an anti-racism campaign in school or at clubs or youth groups.

HOMOPHOBIA
Educational Action Challenging Homophobia (EACH)
Helpline: 0808 100 0143 (Weekdays 9am to 5pm; Saturdays 10am to 12pm)
Web: www.eachaction.org.uk
Email: help@eachaction.org.uk
Offers support, advice and help.

Families and Friends of Lesbians and Gays (FFLAG)

Helpline: 0145 485 2418

Web: www.fflag.org.uk

FFLAG is dedicated to supporting parents and their gay, lesbian and bisexual sons and daughters.

Gay Youth UK

Web: www.gayyouthuk.org.uk

Email: info@gayyouthuk.org.uk

This website aims to provide an online community offering advice, information and support to young lesbian, gay and bisexual people in the UK, as well as those questioning their sexuality.

Joint Action Against Homophobic Bullying (JAAHB)

JAAHB Project

The Intercom Trust

PO Box 285, Exeter

Devon EX1 2YZ

Helpline: 01392 201018

Web: www.intercomtrust.org.uk/bullying or www.pinkparents.org.uk/issue3/3jaahb_project.shtml

A national agency tackling homophobic bullying in schools.

LGBT Youth Scotland Youthline

Helpline: 0845 113 0005 (Tuesdays, 7.30pm to 9pm)

Web: www.lgbtyouth.org.uk

Chat to a trained youth worker about any LGBT (Lesbian, Gay, Bisexual and Transgender) issues that are on your mind. They will also provide information on how to meet other young people across Scotland.

London Lesbian and Gay Switchboard

Helpline: 020 7837 7324

Web: www.llgs.org.uk
Provides an information, support and referral service throughout the UK. You can find out about your local LGBT youth group here.

Safra Project
PO Box 45079
London N4 3YD
Web: www.safraproject.org
The Safra Project is a resource project working on issues relating to lesbian, bisexual and transgender women who identify themselves as Muslim religiously and/or culturally.

Stonewall
46 Grosvenor Gardens
London SW1W 0EB
Tel: 020 7881 9440
Web: www.stonewall.org.uk
Email: info@stonewall.org.uk
Campaigns for the rights of lesbian, gay and bisexual people.

DISABILITY
British Council of Disabled People
Litchurch Plaza, Litchurch Lane
Derby DE24 8AA
Tel: 01332 295551
Web: www.bcodp.org.uk
Email: general@bcodp.org.uk
The council campaigns for the civil rights of disabled people and offers the chance to get involved directly in working together to change society.

Disability Rights Commission

DRC Helpline
FREEPOST MID02164
Stratford upon Avon CV37 9BR
Helpline: 08457 622633
Web: www.drc-gb.org
The helpline offers information on the Disability Discrimination Act and advice if you think you have been discriminated against. Its website also offers detailed advice on your rights and answers to frequently asked questions.

Skill

Helpline: 0800 328 5050
Web: www.skill.org.uk
Skill is a national charity promoting opportunities for young people and adults with any kind of disability in post-16 education, training and employment across the UK.

LEARNING AND COMMUNICATION DIFFERENCES

As-If

Web: www.aspergerinformation.net
Suz's information, advice, support and personal testimony site.

British Dyslexia Association

Helpline: 0118 966 8271 (Monday to Thursday, 10am to 12.30pm and 2pm to 4.30pm)
Web: www.bda-dyslexia.org.uk
Email: helpline@bdadyslexia.org.uk
Information and advice for all those who are in touch with dyslexia for every age group. All calls are treated in confidence.

National Autistic Society (NAS)

Helpline: 0845 070 4004 (Monday to Friday, 10am to 4pm)

Web: www.nas.org.uk

The National Autistic Society champions the rights and interests of all people with autism. Their website includes information about autism and Asperger's syndrome, the NAS and its services and activities. The autism helpline provides confidential help and support for you and your family and can put you in touch with local groups too.

REAL LIFE ISSUES

Real Life Issues are self-help guides offering information and advice on a range of key issues that matter to teenagers. Each book defines the issue, probes the reader's experience of it and offers ways of understanding and coping with it. Written in a lively and accessible style, Real Life Issues aim to demystify the areas that teenagers find hard to talk about, providing honest facts, practical advice, inspirational quotes, positive reassurance, and guidance towards specialist help.

Other titles in the series include:

Real Life Issues: Addictions
Real Life Issues: Bereavement
Real Life Issues: Bullying
Real Life Issues: Confidence & Self-Esteem
Real Life Issues: Coping with Life
Real Life Issues: Eating Disorders
Real Life Issues: Family Break-ups
Real Life Issues: Money
Real Life Issues: Sex & Relationships
Real Life Issues: Stress

REAL LIFE ISSUES:
PREJUDICE

rotman